Stimulating Provision by the Independent Sector

Papers from the 1993 *Caring for People Who Live at Home* Conference

Edited by Isobel Allen, Ailsa Cameron and Liz Perkins

POLICY STUDIES INSTITUTE
London

PUBLISHING

The publishing imprint of the independent
POLICY STUDIES INSTITUTE
100 Park Village East, London NW1 3SR
Telephone: 071-387 2171 Fax: 071-388 0914

© Policy Studies Institute 1994

ISBN 0 85374 612 5

PSI Research Report 774

A CIP catalogue record of this book is available from the British Library.

1 2 3 4 5 6 7 8 9

PSI publications are available from   *1000295559*
BEBC Distribution Ltd
P O Box 1496, Poole, Dorset, BH12 3YD

Books will normally be despatched within 24 hours. Cheques should be made payable to BEBC Distribution Ltd.

Credit card and telephone/fax orders may be placed on the following freephone numbers:

FREEPHONE: 0800 262260
FREEFAX: 0800 262266

Booktrade representation (UK & Eire):
Broadcast Books
24 De Montfort Road, London SW16 1LW
Telephone: 081-677 5129

PSI subscriptions are available from PSI's subscription agent
Carfax Publishing Company Ltd
P O Box 25, Abingdon, Oxford OX14 3UE

Laserset by Policy Studies Institute
Printed in Great Britain by BPC Books and Journals Ltd, Exeter

Preface

This book brings together the papers delivered at the first national *Caring for People who Live at Home* Initiative conference held by Policy Studies Institute at the Queen Elizabeth II conference centre in November 1993. The theme of the conference was stimulating provision by the independent sector.

The interest in the conference was great and it very quickly became over-subscribed. Over 330 people attended the conference with strong representation from the independent sector and health and social services staff.

The aim of the conference was to disseminate information about the work of the Initiative as well as to stimulate debate among practitioners through both plenary and seminar sessions. In addition to the papers which were given in these sessions we have included in these proceedings a summary of the discussions which took place in each of the five seminar groups.

Contents

Preface

Opening Address

John Bowis
Parliamentary Under-Secretary of State, Department of Health

Introduction
I am very happy to be here today to open this first national conference organised as part of the *Caring for People who Live at Home* Initiative. It is gratifying to see so many representatives from local authorities, health authorities and private and voluntary organisations all demonstrating your concern to develop the range of day and domiciliary care services.

Both the independent sector and local authorities face a considerable challenge. To meet that challenge, it is essential that everyone works closely together. Up to now the independent sector has played only a minor role in the provision of such services; but this can change if independent sector agencies seize the opportunities to expand in this area of increasing importance, and local authorities give their active support and encouragement.

One of the main thrusts of our community care reforms is to enable elderly, disabled and other vulnerable people who may wish to do so, to live in their own homes for as long as it is feasible, supported by the appropriate levels and type of care services. For this to be fully effective, and for individuals to have a genuine choice in the type of care they receive, we need a growth in both the variety and quality of non-residential services. And the new agencies, given the inevitable uncertainties of a new market, need nurture and careful management. They cannot develop in a vacuum of lack of information and support. Flexibility and adapting to the new culture is essential. Above all they need to be consulted about and wholly aware of the specifications from local authorities for such services.

Setting up the Initiative

Because of the important role we see the independent sector playing in the provision of day and domiciliary services, and because we do not underestimate the complexities, the government has committed around £6 million to this three-year Initiative which is designed to identify ways in which day and domiciliary services can be developed to:

- increase the range and responsiveness of services;

- reflect users' and carers' needs;

- improve services which might help prevent people having to be admitted to residential care unnecessarily; and

- stimulate a mixed economy of care by encouraging local authorities to work closely with the independent sector.

The response from local authorities to the announcement about the Initiative was impressive – over 150 proposals, amounting to around £17 million. This reflected the importance authorities rightly attach to developing the range of day and domiciliary services locally. It was a very difficult task to arrive at the final selection which includes an interactive range of different approaches. And my predecessor announced, just a year ago, details of the 15 local authorities which had been invited to take part in what is called the *Caring for People who Live at Home* Initiative.

Details of some of the projects

All of the authorities are beginning to progress with some interesting ideas and it is good to see the different approaches they are adopting. You are here today to share experience and the lessons emerging, so I will not dwell on the details. But I will mention just a few examples. Shropshire has set up an Enterprise Agency to develop the independent sector. This can work well as it combines business advice and acumen with local authority knowledge about local need, and about existing service provision or service gaps. Rochdale is working with seven nursing homes to provide outreach services for people with mental health problems.

Barnsley's bid did not include provision for funding actual service developments, but only for development staff. The development officer has therefore sought to stimulate projects which are immediately income generating, or has helped to secure external funding for projects. Much of the work aims to change attitudes and practices within the social services department in order to help the department meet the new demands of community care.

Other work under the Initiative

There are already three significant publications linked into the Initiative. In October, the Social Services Inspectorate produced *Developing Quality Standards for Home Support Services* as part of their Inspecting for Quality series. Home support services are the cornerstone of effective community care packages enabling people to live independently in the community. I know that many of the authorities taking part in the Initiative are trying to develop such services and will find this document of great value. The handbook suggests key principles to help all those with an interest in or responsibility for such services to recognise and achieve quality. As such it will be of interest to both purchasers and providers of home support services. As the mixed economy of care develops and more services are provided by the independent sector we need to give particular attention to ensuring the quality of all services. The handbook provides a framework for developing standards.

The Inspectorate also commissioned KPMG to produce a manual to assist smaller independent sector providers of residential care in understanding the issues involved in diversifying to develop services to help users and carers living in their own homes. The report, which I know you will be hearing more about today, was also published recently. It is a manual for providers of care, but it also has important messages for purchasers of care. As part of the process of developing their understanding of the issues, KPMG visited five local authority areas and talked to purchasers as well as providers.

Some of the key messages that emerged from these discussions were highlighted in the Chief Inspector's letter to local authorities which accompanied the manual. I should like to reinforce those messages. They were:

- In order to manage diversification effectively, purchasers and providers must plan developments and projects together and engage in a creative dialogue.

- Information is a vital resource in assisting providers to diversify.

• There needs to be development and sharing of service design principles with providers.

• Service specifications should be published and intended outcomes for users and carers should be shared so that providers can innovate to achieve these.

• Diversification may sometimes require resources, including help with start up or development costs, and purchasers will want to consider ways of promoting pilot schemes and of monitoring and developing progress.

The third publication, from the Policy Studies Institute, is Diana Leat's book, *The Development of Community Care by the Independent Sector,* which is published today, and which will be the subject of discussion later this morning.

Direction and extra funding

As I have said, the new community care arrangements offer great opportunities and challenges for expanding day and domiciliary care. The independent sector has not so far been a major provider of such services to local authorities. This needs to change. More providers will mean more choice and services which are more likely to be tailored to individual clients' needs. Authorities should therefore be looking increasingly to purchase day and domiciliary services from a range of different organisations. Many care home owners will be seeking to diversify. From wherever they come, new providers need information and encouragement to do so.

Many of you will have heard our announcement in Parliament in October 1994, and at the Social Services Conference in Birmingham, that the Special Transitional Grant, which was to be £716m for 1994-95 is to be increased by £20m to £736m and will be increased by £30m for 1995-96, from £618m to £648m. These increases will help social services authorities to arrange for more home care and respite care. This means a ring-fenced budget may rise to nearly £2 billion over the first three year of community care implementation.

I receive contradictory messages about the potential for alternative sources of day and domiciliary care. On the one hand I am told by some authorities that the 85 per cent condition is difficult to meet because there is no supply. On the other hand I am told by the independent sector that they are ready and waiting to branch out into new services, if only specifications for tendering were available.

I think what is required is more openness and certainty. We are therefore discussing with the Local Authority Associations, and others, the possibility of issuing a directive which would require authorities to issue clear statements of their plans for expanding the range of non-residential service providers with whom they deal. In this way authorities will be clear what they are setting out to do and potential providers will know what the opportunities are likely to be.

Other authorities' work

Although 15 authorities were selected to take part in the Initiative, it was evident from the applications that came from almost every authority that new ideas and ways of providing services are widespread. I have heard of a local pub in a rural community being used as a day centre and luncheon club for elderly people, with the landlord being under contract to provide the room and food; and an authority placing contracts with home owners and so being able to expand its night sitting and out of hours services, by drawing on independent sector residential care staff who are used to working out of hours. I very much welcome these developments.

Conclusion

Finally I would like to say that the 15 authorities taking part in the *Caring for People who Live at Home* Initiative have my full interest and we can look forward to hearing more about their successes and lessons learnt, hopefully largely good practice but including perhaps in some cases how things can go wrong, as the Initiative progresses. The work of the 15 authorities, whilst exciting in itself, is only part of the Initiative. It needs opportunities such as this to influence and provide others with details of the innovative approaches and diversity of experiences which the authorities are encountering. One of the main objectives of the Initiative was for the participating authorities to share with others their experiences and the lessons being learnt through their work and the new skills required. This is one of the crucial roles of the Policy Studies Institute: to disseminate information through the Newsletter, brochures and other means. I hope that this conference will be a valuable part of that dissemination process, and that the experiences of the participating authorities may give you the encouragement and inspiration to continue in your work towards the mixed economy of care to which we are committed.

Caring for People who Live at Home:
the First Year

Isobel Allen
Policy Studies Institute

I would like to start this paper by giving you some of the background to the *Caring for People who Live at Home* Initiative. You have already heard how and why it was set up and its aims and objectives, but I will give you some more information on how the participating authorities were selected and the role of Policy Studies Institute. I will go on to talk about the 15 participating authorities and some of the themes which emerged in their original bids and which have run through the development of the projects. I will look at their work over the past year and at some of their achievements so far and the ingredients for success. I will conclude by looking at some of the problems they have faced in getting the show on the road, relating them to the problems facing all projects which are set up as 'demonstration projects', and putting them in the context of the wider issues which have faced all authorities and the independent sector in tackling the question of developing the 'mixed economy' of care.

I want to stress that the Initiative was not set up to be a beauty contest. We are not looking for a Miss – or Mr – Caring for People who Live at Home. We are looking for examples of good practice, of bright ideas, of things that work well, of ways of cooperation and collaboration that were unheard of before this year. But at the same time, we must not neglect to note problems, unintended consequences, and constraints which must be removed if the aims of the Initiative are to be achieved. The tone of this paper will be positive, but it would be wrong to assume that there are no problems to be solved, both by local authorities in developing their supporting and enabling role, and by private and voluntary agencies in developing their providing role.

The Caring for People who Live at Home Initiative

The *Caring for People who Live at Home* Initiative was announced by the Department of Health in January 1992 with the aim of stimulating the provision of day and domiciliary services within the independent sector – the private and voluntary sector. We have heard that it was intended to increase the numbers and types of providers, reflect the needs of users and carers, and improve services generally in order to prevent unnecessary or premature admission to residential care.

The process of shortlisting from the 150 or so bids took place in the autumn of 1992, with a panel made up of Department of Health staff, representatives of the Local Authority Associations, the Joint Advisory Group of Domiciliary Care Associations and Policy Studies Institute. Each project was assessed in relation to the following criteria:

- its ability to stimulate development in the independent sector in ways which were new and innovative;

- the presence of clearly stated and realistic objectives and an indication of sustainability in the long term;

- the potential value of the project to other authorities;

- the extent to which it involved coordination and cooperation between local authorities and other agencies.

In addition, attention was paid to achieving a good geographical spread, an urban-rural mix, and a mix of types of authority, for example, London borough, county council and metropolitan borough.

The selection of 15 authorities was announced in November 1992 and funding is available until March 1995.The participating authorities are Barnsley, Cambridgeshire, Camden, Devon, Essex, Gloucestershire, Hammersmith and Fulham, Lewisham, Liverpool, Newham, North Yorkshire, Richmond upon Thames, Rochdale, Sandwell and Shropshire. They all have displays at the conference giving full details of their work and a brief account of the aims and scope of the plans of each these authorities is given in the *Caring for People who Live at Home* Initiative brochure. In a moment I will talk about the work being undertaken by the participating authorities, but first I would like to outline briefly the role of Policy Studies Institute in the Initiative.

Policy Studies Institute's role

Policy Studies Institute is responsible for the overall coordination and management of the Initiative on behalf of the Department of Health. PSI is an independent research institute with a long record of research in health and social care and has for many years had close contact both with the Department of Health and the Association of Directors of Social Services. We also have experience of managing other projects similar to the present Initiative – for example the *Caring in Homes Initiative* and the *National Disability Information Project*, both funded by the Department of Health.

The role of the PSI team is to ensure that the work of the Initiative is carried out efficiently and effectively so that its aims are achieved. We have three main functions:

- managing and coordinating the Initiative as a whole;
- disseminating the experience gained through the local projects as widely as possible;
- evaluating the impact of the Initiative and the work of the local projects.

We have an Advisory Group made up of representatives from a number of organisations with a particular interest in the work of the Initiative – the Department of Health, the Social Services Inspectorate, the Local Authority Associations, the Joint Advisory Group of Domiciliary Care Agencies, the United Kingdom Home Care Association and representatives of users' and carers' organisations. Advisory Group members play a key role in advising us on the management of the Initiative and members are chairing most of the seminar sessions led by the participating authorities this afternoon.

The work of the participating authorities

I would like to turn now to the work of the participating authorities. The *Caring for People who Live at Home* Initiative is designed to stimulate new thinking and innovation. The money was made available for fresh initiatives and to encourage the independent sector to enter or develop services where they had been underdeveloped before. It was not designed to help to provide 'more of the same' or

9

to fill gaps in provision which are the current responsibility of the local authorities. Most importantly, perhaps, the Initiative was designed to stimulate projects and services which are sustainable in the long term. In other words, there has to be a strong indication that, at the end of the Initiative, services which have been stimulated, encouraged or initiated will be able to continue because someone is going to purchase them.

There are certain underlying patterns and themes by which the activities of the participating authorities can be grouped. The 15 projects are surprisingly different from one another but we have identified certain basic themes of work and development. These are enterprise development; rural development; ethnic minorities; diversification; and training.

You will see that we have identified three of them as particularly important for this afternoon's seminar sessions – enterprise development, rural development and the development of services for ethnic minorities. Representatives from authorities which have been particularly active in these areas will be discussing their experience. And Peter Whittingham is going to speak later this morning about the research and development exercise he carried out with funding from the *Caring for People who Live at Home* Initiative on diversification.

I should like to give you some examples of what is going on under these themes, and in doing so I will talk about some of the achievements of authorities in the Initiative. I will also give some indication of why they are important for the development of the independent sector. I should stress that the examples are only indicative, and that just because I have not mentioned an authority under a particular theme or development it is not because they are not doing a great job.

- *Enterprise development*: these authorities are aiming to work closely with the business community or with particular agencies, offering advice and practical help in starting up or developing business skills. Probably foremost among these has been Shropshire which has set up a Social Care Enterprise Agency which provides information to potential providers about the local authority's purchasing intentions and current services, as well as offering financial support to new services through pump-priming funding. In addition, Shropshire and Cambridgeshire offer advice on business skills to potential providers and help them develop business plans, and North Yorkshire is arranging to set up sessions with specialist business advisers for potential providers. There can be no doubt that business skills are crucial in ensuring the long-term viability of independent sector services. But it must be noted that stimulation of private enterprise has not been a traditional function of local authority staff. These skills have to be developed in-house or recruited or bought in. The Initiative is identifying and underlining the need for these special skills within local authorities in helping to develop and nurture business skills within the independent sector, and the participating authorities are giving some clear examples of how to go about it.

- *Rural development*: the specific aim of these authorities is to stimulate development of the independent sector in rural areas which are often not well served either by the statutory or independent sectors at present. Among these authorities are Cambridgeshire, Devon, Essex and Gloucestershire. Perhaps one of the most important factors to mention here is that rural areas may be very different from one another, particularly in the types of services which are already available, even in one authority, like Devon which has two projects in different parts of the county. It is far too simplistic to say that rural areas require a particular type of response, and no doubt this will be discussed in detail in the seminars. There are particular problems in that users of services may be very dispersed, and different models of stimulation of the independent sector from those used in urban areas are certainly called for in rural areas. There is certainly evidence that trying to develop services only for one particular group of users may not work, and that a more generic approach to the provision of services is in order.

- *Ethnic minorities*: there are a series of projects aimed specifically at stimulating the provision of services for members of ethnic minorities – particularly by members of those groups themselves. Two of the authorities, Hammersmith and Fulham and Newham, have designed their projects around the stimulation of services for ethnic minority users by providers from ethnic minorities, and Sandwell and Liverpool are both developing the provision of services for specific ethnic minority groups. Other authorities are pump-priming or working with organisations providing services to ethnic minority communities. For example Camden has some innovative schemes specifically designed for the Jewish and Chinese communities, and Cambridgeshire has stimulated provision for Italian and Afro-Caribbean groups.

- *Diversification*: these are authorities which are aiming to stimulate existing agencies, like private or voluntary residential or nursing homes or other agencies, to provide a variety of other services from their base. Rochdale's project is based on seven nursing homes diversifying into an outreach carer respite services, aimed at those who care for people with mental health problems in old age. Shropshire has also worked with more than 36 care homes and nursing homes interested in diversifying into respite care, day care or home care services. Eight homes have now applied for inclusion on the approved provider list for home care. Camden are working with housing associations and Gloucestershire with sheltered housing schemes.

- *Training*: only one authority – Lewisham – put up a project in which all the money went into a training initiative – running a BTec approved course at Lewisham College in business and care skills for potential independent providers. But other authorities are exploring ways of developing training for providers – for example North Yorkshire is holding business development seminars and Newham is proposing to hold training sessions with providers. Gloucestershire will be holding four workshops with providers, covering such subjects as business planning and information technology.

These are the main themes underlining the work of the participating authorities, but cutting across these themes, there are a variety of activities: mapping the market; establishment of consultative/advisory groups; contact with providers/potential providers; pump-priming activites; service development; and practical services for relatively low priority groups.

- *Mapping the market*: an examination or investigation of the market for services which could be provided by the independent sector. This has been done in a variety of ways, ranging from North Yorkshire's commissioning of a wide-scale research report from the University of York, to Hammersmith and Fulham and Newham which commissioned a detailed analysis of discrete parts of the market, through to Cambridgeshire which sent questionnaires to all known providers, to the search by a number of authorities, like Camden and Gloucestershire, through all known providers and the yellow pages and other directories to identify potential providers of services, to North Yorkshire again who advertised in the local press. I suppose that one of the things which surprised us was how little most authorities actually knew about potential providers within the independent sector. Most authorities were really starting virtually from scratch in this respect.

- *Establishment of consultative/advisory groups*: a number of the participating authorities have set up consultation exercises with potential providers and/or with users of services, like Hammersmith and Fulham and Newham again. Most have made sure that they have an advisory or steering group, sometimes for the project as a whole and sometimes for various parts of their project. There can be little doubt that an advisory or steering group is an important factor, particularly in validating the selection of providers for funding under the Initiative money and the placing of contracts.

- *Contact with providers/potential providers*: this has varied from involving providers or potential providers in consultative/advisory groups, to setting up focus groups, to following up the mapping the market exercise in a number of ways. There has then been a variety of approaches: going out to tender, inviting expressions of interest, revisiting 'preferred providers' and the 'tap on the shoulder' approach favoured by Barnsley. There are many lessons to be learnt from the various ways in which the participating authorities have gone about setting up or funding services under the Initiative. Diana Leat will be talking about some of the potential problems, but I am sure that the authorities themselves will be able to give examples during the seminars this afternoon. There are certainly many issues surrounding contracting and quality standards which have emerged from the growing contact between the participating authorities and the independent sector, and it is interesting how some project teams have very quickly developed knowledge and expertise within their projects which has apparently been rather hard to access within their authorities.

- *Pump-priming activities*: projects designed to put some start-up money into new and innovative initiatives which otherwise might not have got off the ground, particularly those offered by agencies with which authorities have had no previous contact. Cambridgeshire, Camden, Devon, Hammersmith and Fulham, Newham, North Yorkshire, Richmond upon Thames and Shropshire are all authorities which are developing such activities and using their funding at least partly in this way.

- *Service development*: some authorities identified very specific services which they wished to develop under the Initiative. These were sometimes new services which were thought to need longer-term funding than simply pump-priming, while others were services which were already up-and-running but were thought to need additional funds to make them more viable in the longer-term. Essentially they were often part of a wider service development, as in Essex, Gloucestershire, Liverpool, Rochdale and Sandwell. The aim of the Essex project is to develop day, domiciliary and respite services in a rural area where a residential home was being closed. Part of Liverpool's project is to develop individual supported living arrangements enabling people with a learning disability to live where and how they wished. Sandwell's aim has been to develop a practical needs-led support service available day and night for older people in the early stages of dementia and for black elderly people.

- *Practical services for relatively low priority groups*: for example gardening services or minor repair services for elderly people. This kind of service may come well below the eligibility criteria in terms of needs assessment, and not even creep into the type of domiciliary services which are now regarded as preventative rather than essential in keeping people out of residential care. And yet, anyone who has done research on the needs of users or analysed user satisfaction can confirm that the availability of these services may well be the crucial factor which determines whether people feel they can continue to live in the community with dignity. North Yorkshire, Camden, Devon and Essex have been looking at the development of such services, and Gloucestershire has stimulated a handy person's service in a sheltered housing scheme.

Problems

I said at the beginning of this paper that my main aim was to be positive, but it would be unrealistic, and I think, unfair to the participating authorities, to pretend that the development of this Initiative has been without problems. At the end of the day, we are evaluating the Initiative and drawing lessons from the experience of the participating authorities. There are a number of factors which have affected the progress of the Initiative so far and I think it would be useful to share some of these with you, since many of you will have had the same experience. Some are perhaps specific to the Initiative itself, but others have a more general application.

Getting started

First of all, there was a problem for all the participating authorities in getting started. The announcement of the successful authorities in the bidding process was made just over a year ago – in November 1992. The funding period was for two and a half years from then until March 1995. It was perhaps not surprising that some of the authorities felt overwhelmed by their success, particularly since it came shortly before they were due to implement the NHS and Community Care Act on April 1st, 1993. There can be no doubt that some of the authorities were not really geared up to getting the Initiative off the ground at the same time as implementing the community care reforms, particularly since key staff were involved in both exercises. A slow start was the result for most authorities – and a very slow start was the result for some.

The ones which got going most quickly were, interestingly, those using very different approaches: first those which used existing staff with clearly defined duties to get the projects off the ground. These authorities usually had a very tight management steer and interest at a high level. The others which got off to a quick start were those which advertised for staff very quickly and then set up a project which was almost at arm's length from the authority, leaving the staff who were closely involved in the community care implementation to get on with that, while making sure that the project staff had high-level support.

It must be stressed that the participating authorities were all starting from very different bases, particularly as far as the development of the independent sector was concerned. In some authorities, particularly the Inner London and metropolitan boroughs, the independent sector was restricted mainly to voluntary organisations, and the private sector hardly existed, not only in day and domiciliary care provision but also in residential care provision, whereas some other authorities had huge numbers of private residential and nursing homes, many of whose proprietors were very concerned about their future after 1 April 1993. Others had well-developed links with voluntary organisations, but were running into numerous concerns about future funding relationships and changing roles.

There can be no doubt that the problems facing Barnsley, for example, with virtually no independent sector, were very different from those facing neighbouring North Yorkshire which could be described as having a very active independent sector.

Staffing

The participating authorities took different approaches to the staffing of these projects. The majority of them employed new or redeployed staff as project team leaders, and this has not been without problems, mainly because most were slow to advertise and some had difficulties in attracting the right candidates, mainly because of the unique combination of skills required, which were not generally associated with social services departments. This has contributed to the slow start for many of the authorities.

Management and support

I have indicated that the projects which got off the ground quickly benefited from top management support and involvement. It is clearly an essential ingredient in the success of initiatives of this kind that such support is available and continuing. New and innovative projects are not easy to fit into a structure, particularly if they have a limited life. They have to be given credibility by top management interest which is sustained beyond the initial thrill of getting the money in competition with everyone else. If these projects are to succeed, particularly since the roles undertaken by project staff are usually very different from those traditionally undertaken in social services departments, there must be good management and guidance at a senior level. The work of the projects must be given validity within the organisation and they must not just be regarded as a bit of extra jam which will disappear in a couple of years. The developmental work of these projects today will be the staple fare of many social services departments tomorrow. It is important that this is recognised.

Position of the project teams in the structure

I have suggested that the position of the project teams within the local authority structure is important, although, as I have noted, no one model was necessarily better than another in getting the Initiative started. However, there are certainly indications that some project teams are able to function more smoothly than others. It does seem necessary for the project team leader to have very close links with the purchasers, so that the work of the project is informed by the purchasing intentions of the authority, and, equally important, so that the project team can make a contribution to the purchasing plans of the authority.

It also seems essential for the project team leader to have close contact with contracting and legal departments and with business development departments of the local authority. We have seen some floundering around because staff have found it so difficult to get advice or even access to key departments like these. It really should not be necessary for the project teams to be reinventing wheels which others with more dedicated time and greater expertise have invented so well before them.

Getting going with innovation

Probably the most successful innovations are introduced by people with a very clear and personal idea of what they want to achieve. These are sometimes referred to as 'heroic pioneers' who have a strong determination to succeed. They have often been nurturing their idea for years, building contacts, establishing networks and creating the right seed-bed for their ideas to take root in. None of the projects has really been in this position, and I think it must be recognised how difficult it is to be a pioneer – heroic or otherwise. However, one of the most interesting aspects of the Initiative from PSI's point of view, has been to observe how some project staff, however late they have been appointed, have really seized the opportunity and forged ahead with imagination and verve. Even if they are not particularly heroic, they have really put down their markers in a short space of time, and who knows what they will achieve by the end of the Initiative.

Purchasing intentions

One of the main themes running through the work of the participating authorities has been the requirement that the services stimulated or set up through the Initiative should be sustainable and viable in the long-term. It is simply not feasible that services should be funded under the Initiative and then cease in 1995. Someone has got to purchase them.

This Initiative has really demonstrated the importance of making sure that local authority purchasing plans are communicated to the independent sector, not only to known and trusted providers but also to potential and unknown providers. It has shown how important it is for local authorities to identify the needs for services, to identify the gaps, to identify the services which could fill these gaps and to stimulate independent sector providers to meet these needs. It has demonstrated that potential providers will come forward if they are encouraged and nurtured and helped, but it has also demonstrated that short-term encouragement and funding are not enough. Before providers take a risk, they need some indication that their services will be purchased, and for this they need to have some trust in the purchasing intentions of the local authority. Conversely, of course, the local authority needs to have trust in the capacity and ability of independent sector providers to deliver quality services for vulnerable people. The Initiative has offered the opportunity for purchasers and providers to have a real relationship and partnership – and it is undoubtedly partnership which will be the key factor in the development of the independent sector.

Short-term 'demonstration' projects

A general rule is that every project of this kind, which has short-term funding, a limited life and is set up as a 'demonstration' project, has particular problems of its own. It is usually starting from scratch, often with new staff on short-term contracts, or redeployed staff, who are expected to initiate innovative projects, often without strong management support structures or even clear lines of responsibility.

The projects are set up to demonstrate something and the staff are expected to achieve their objectives, which may well have been laid down by someone else who was not going to have to achieve them. They are often under the scrutiny of an external evaluator, so that they will be expected to maintain good internal monitoring procedures as well as working in a new, exciting and innovative way to stimulate others to do the same.

There is no doubt that there are problems in running demonstration projects – but there are also enormous opportunities. The scrutiny can be turned to good effect, the exposure is great, and if you succeed, so are the rewards. Even if every move you make is not incredibly successful, at least you will have been in the vanguard of changing cultures in a way which few have done. There is a lot for everyone to learn – from your achievements and from your struggles.

Conclusions

I have only been able to take you on a quick tour around the participating authorities in the *Caring for People who Live at Home* Initiative and to identify some of the ways in which they have approached their task, their achievements and the ingredients for success. I have tried to give you an overview of the Initiative as a whole. You will be hearing much more from the authorities themselves later in the day about their work, and you will be able to relate it to your own experience and the expectations of the Government.

I am sure that most of the participating authorities in the present Initiative have benefited by being able to share their experience with others taking part in the Initiative, and as the projects begin to take shape and get off the ground, Policy Studies Institute intends to disseminate more widely the successes and achievements of the participating authorities. But, as I said at the beginning, nobody can pretend that it is an easy task to change custom and practice which have been accepted for a long time in local authorities and the independent sector alike.

Caring for People who Live at Home: Ways Forward

Diana Leat
Author of *The Development of Community Care by the Independent Sector*

Making care happen

Voluntary and private organisations do exist and they are providing care for people who live at home. In some authorities their numbers are growing. If we look at research conducted in the last ten years into various initiatives designed to stimulate community care there are a number of common themes. These are themes which have been and will be touched on throughout the conference. Making new initiatives in community care happen requires political and managerial commitment to making them work and confidence that they will work. New initiatives require time – more time than might have been thought necessary at the outset; and that takes us back to commitment and confidence to keep going even when things seem to be progressing all too slowly. New initiatives require money and resources, especially in the early years – again, perhaps more than might have been hoped. They also require people to provide care. Organisations do not provide care: people do. We must pay attention to the needs of volunteers and paid care workers; we must minimise the costs and maximise the satisfactions of providing care. Information and communication between purchasers, providers and users are essential to the development of new community care initiatives. Finally, new initiatives require commitment and support from top management, clear lines of responsibility and accountability at all levels.

Encouraging day and domiciliary care also, of course, requires commitment and confidence, and all of the other ingredients above, within the independent sector. But, at present, some independent sector organisations have to be seen in the context of purchasers' needs because, in some respects, they are created by purchasers' needs which are, in turn, created by the requirements of the NHS and Community Care Act and subsequent guidance. Whether or not independent sector uncertainties are a product of purchasers' needs, they will have to be resolved in the context of those needs.

Purchasers' needs

In theory purchasers need:

- choice of low-cost high quality providers to ensure competition at the contract stage;

- on-going choice of low-cost high quality providers to ensure flexibility over time to meet new needs, to avoid monopoly suppliers and to provide continuing competition;

- the ability to ensure value-for-money, drive 'hard bargains' and contain costs within pre-determined budgets;

- to have trust in the ability and reliability of suppliers;

- to exercise control over who is served and how;

- to maintain standards and accountability via easily applied, common procedures;

- to achieve managerial and administrative efficiency throughout the contracting process from initial selection to on-going maintenance of standards.

Purchasers' needs may contain some internal contradictions in practice, if not in theory. In addition the needs of purchasers may conflict with the needs of suppliers. Choice and competition are the dominant words of the Act. In its implementation the word conflict may need to be added, and compromise may be the ingredient essential in achieving its goals.

21

Independent sector needs and uncertainties
Lack of information, understanding and skills
Larger organisations, or those which are part of a wider network, may have access to the information and skills necessary for contracting. If individuals, smaller or more isolated organisations are to become involved, purchasing authorities may need to make a concerted effort to provide information, support and skills. But this raises a number of questions. Do all authorities have staff with an adequate understanding of the voluntary and private sectors to perform this function well? Will staff be prepared to commit time and resources to an exercise which looks very like old style community development and grant-aid and may not fit very comfortably in the new contract culture? Is it fair, or an efficient use of resources, to encourage smaller organisations to become involved in a competitive exercise in which they may have little chance of success or security?

Political uncertainty
Voluntary and private sector organisations may see contracting out as a political exercise subject to considerable uncertainty. Private sector organisations in particular may believe that this is not a level playing field, that the voluntary sector has the ideological and fiscal wind on its side, as well as indirect financial and other subsidies from parent bodies and supporters, and a long-standing relationship with the referee.

Financial uncertainty
Financial uncertainty for providers is built into contracting via the emphasis on competition and flexibility for purchasers. There is uncertainty about the size of the market – how much home care will local authorities purchase? Then there is uncertainty about the number of private and voluntary competitors. It is not just a matter of how big the home care cake will be, but also one of how many pieces will be cut and how big each slice will be. Trying to keep the metaphor going, will the cake be ice-cream gateau which melts into nothing, or wedding cake which keeps for years? Will the number of care-hours purchased be reliable over time? If not, this will play havoc with an organisation's allocation of overheads and may make the difference between survival and collapse. This raises a wider issue about costs to be covered and

contract terms; the type of contract may increase or decrease financial uncertainty for the provider.

Then there are the direct and indirect costs of becoming involved in contracting: time and energy, fees for specialist organisations, and so on. There are also anxieties and uncertainties about VAT for private sector organisations, and for voluntary organisations the effects of contracting on donations of time and money. And, of course, there are uncertainties and anxieties about insurance and legal costs.

All of these uncertainties may be exacerbated by uncertainties in the wider financial context. A small change in, say, national insurance rates or in the policy of banks may hit small organisations very hard.

Entry costs and risks

Under this heading there are uncertainties concerning direct and opportunity costs in time spent planning, acquiring information, negotiating, buying in specialist skills – very possibly all for nothing.

I mentioned above that purchasers need to trust suppliers. Organisations entering the market face a double problem. They need to enter the market to establish a track record and generate trust. But at the same time they need some guarantee of business before it is worthwhile incurring the costs of entry.

Anxiety and uncertainty concerning regulation

This covers a range of issues. There are anxieties and uncertainties concerning likely requirements for registration. If registration is required locally, what will be the conditions? Then there is a set of issues to do with regulation of the use of volunteers, employed and self-employed care workers. This is a very complex issue which is closely connected with VAT. But if forced to become employers with all the legal, financial and administrative costs entailed, many smaller organisations may choose to leave the market. Regulation is, of course, also related to organisational discretion. Some organisations fear that greater regulation will damage the provision of what they see as quality care; others fear that regulation may change the whole structure and ethos of the organisation (the use of volunteers for example).

Effects on charitable mission and independence

Charities may have a number of particular anxieties. Many will want to retain some control over who is served and how, not least to ensure that what they do fits their charitable mission. The new 'openness' about rationing poses important moral dilemmas for charities. Historically their role has been to help those outside the state welfare net. Should they now become involved in helping (only) those who fall inside? Charging is another difficult moral issue for many charities, but also one of considerable wider significance in relation to the very notion of a voluntary sector distinct from the private sector. Local authority policies on charging and levels of charging seem especially likely to change with the political composition of the authority; this uncertainty may exacerbate other anxieties. There are also practical issues in charging. Organisations may find themselves charging users referred by one social service department, charging users at a lower rate referred by another, and not charging users at all if they come via some other route – all for exactly the same service.

These are some issues of particular concern to charities but the wider issue of independence and interference in management of the organisation may be of concern to both private and voluntary organisations. Voluntary organisations have always jealously guarded their independence – or the principle at least. Private sector organisations have probably taken independence for granted. Both types of organisation may be anxious that the line between contract provision and take-over is a fine one.

These issues, among others, are discussed in more detail in the review *The Development of Community Care by the Independent Sector* (Leat, 1993). One aim of this presentation, and the review, has been to contribute to a constructive debate concerning means of resolving, overcoming or circumventing openly acknowledged difficulties: a debate which seeks ways forward.

References
Leat, D., *The Development of Community Care by the Independent Sector,* Policy Studies Institute, 1993

Managing Diversification: Success Factors for Purchasers and Providers

Peter Whittingham
Executive Consultant, KPMG Peat Marwick

Diversification is currently rather voguish and certainly much quoted in the care home trade press and discussed amongst development managers and purchasers in local authorities.

Diversification is a means and not an end. The end is better quality care to allow individuals who require support greater choice and independence to live at home in ordinary ways. Diversification must be driven by outcomes. The key question and one that goes to the heart of the community care market is whether some existing residential care providers can make a switch into other industries. I want in this discussion:

- to highlight the reasons why under certain conditions, diversification is of interest to purchasers and providers, and why it might consume strategic planning and purchasing time as well as business planning effort;

- to report on the findings of a Social Services Inspectorate (SSI) commissioned study of diversification undertaken earlier this year (KPMG Peat Marwick, 1993). One of the outputs of that study is currently available as a manual to assist care home providers consider reasons for diversification and ways of achieving it;

- to look ahead in community care and seek to assess what the market in diversified services might look like in two or three years time, once the impact of Special Transitional Grant is on the wane and the distribution of central government funding through SSA reasserts its grip.

In addressing these issues I will draw upon four main sources: our consultancy work with health and local authorities who are seeking to influence the community care market; our work for the SSI which brought us into contact with diversification developments across the country; other SSI work notably by David Raw and Colin Shipley in the South West of England, and, increasingly, our work with providers of diversified services.

I do not say manage the community care market because I do not think the community care market can necessarily be easily managed, for it is an external as well as an internal market with real, rather than created, market forces. What happens in the external economy, for example the autumn budget, will have a significant impact upon care home activities and business. This is different from the NHS internal market.

Much of what I say concerns services for older people, and at one level, only in certain parts of the country where the residential care home or nursing home supply vastly exceeds demand. Much will depend on the arrangement and deployment of other providers. For other user groups, younger disabled people or people with mental health problems, the issue is often not diversification from a residential base but the creation of ordinary local services of any kind in a locality. The issue is one of undersupply not oversupply.

Why is diversification on the agenda now?
By diversification I mean building on a core business a range of differing (though often related) products as a way of expanding a business or reducing reliance on core services alone. In community care this means moving from solely residential care to exploring care packages to support people in their own homes and assist carers.

This draws out the two meanings of diversification. Firstly, diversification as a positive strategy for expanding a business or secondly defensive diversification, where reliance on core services is sought to be reduced. Nothing spectacular, nothing particularly complex, yet all the evidence is that *currently,* and I emphasise currently, some homes are finding it difficult, whilst others have already achieved it or decided it is not worth the investment, or funders the risks entailed.

I should also have said at the beginning that my remarks are based around efforts by the independent sector to diversify, by private for-profit, and voluntary or not-for-profit groups. This is somewhat paradoxical for one of the implications of the income support funding for independent homes in the 1980s was the reduction in pressure upon local and health authority resources i.e. beds. This allowed health authorities to redefine their purchasing strategies and to consolidate around health care, particularly acute care, and diversify out of the long term or continuing care business in some parts of the country. In some areas this has resulted in greater investment in community health services.

Similarly, local authorities took the opportunity to review the role of residential care, particularly for older people, and it allowed them to reduce bed numbers and add on day, domiciliary, respite care. Many elderly persons' homes now stand as a model of diversified services, serving not just the needs of their residents but of service users and carers living locally. Whilst these changes were the result of medium term service planning rather than the operation of a market in residential care services, the opportunity to refocus or diversify resulted from changes in the external independent sector market.

So, diversification can be done. It is important now for a number of reasons. For purchasers it is important:

1. To provide services to people in their own homes which will meet their needs and those of their carers. In short, a policy aim of *Caring for People* and a possible local purchasing strategy.

2. To increase the volume of domiciliary alternatives that can be packaged by care managers – basically, a capacity and supply aim. If there is a problem at present it is lack of supply, in sufficient volume in certain areas. Rural areas, for example, experience particular problems with domiciliary services.

3. To shift the balance in the mixed economy of domiciliary care. Independent domiciliary providers are not present in volume terms, compared to public sector services. Authorities will have differing views on the appropriateness of the balance. This is a mixed economy aim and the potential benefits are to quality and price and greater competition amongst providers. This mix in the domiciliary care market must be contrasted with the broad spread of provision in the residential care sector. This mix, it can be argued, has been instrumental in securing greater quality, choice and better prices for users and purchasers. There is also an interesting issue as to whether there is in fact a community care

market covering residential and domiciliary sectors or whether these are indeed different market segments comprising different industries. If they are different industries, then the ability of providers in one segment to move into provision of another segment could be called into question. Certainly this division has always been apparent in the local authority management of services, and Diana Leat makes the point strongly that the residential care sector should not be seen necessarily as a model for the development of the domiciliary care sector (Leat, 1993).

4. As a means of managing down an over-supply of residential or nursing home beds in an area, offering ways out of mainstream residential provision and into community care services – a market development aim. This means of managing down and at the same time managing up the supply of non-residential care could be seen as very neat and convenient for purchasers – hence the attraction to them.

5. As a means of capitalising on the windfall gain of STG. This cannot be committed to long term placement support but can be used to invest in organisations which may provide supply in the future. There is some indication that special transitional grants are having a number of short term converse affects. These include the transfer of residents from local authority homes to the independent sector and the creation off community care trusts from local government services in order to qualify for STG support.

For providers, diversification is important for other reasons – some of them the reverse of purchaser concerns.

1. Survival and diversity in adversity or what I have called defensive diversification (Whittingham, 1993). Creating alternative sources of income within the community care business does mean a major shift of emphasis from a bed-based concern to a community-based concern requiring new and significant managerial skills. In areas of structural decline in the residential care market diversification can be a survival strategy. By structural decline I mean those areas that will see a progressive withdrawal of publicly funded support, as larger sums of STG switches to smaller SSAs.

2. As a means of expanding a business, where a home has a competitive advantage, for example, in a rural location with few

other homes nearby; or a particular set of skills e.g. nursing, when surrounded by residential care providers, these can be applied locally off-site to advantage. One area of business expansion by some already successful owners is in franchise or consultancy packages to other homes to assist diversification. There are at least four advertising nationally at present. These appear to offer a range of services built around community alarm schemes amongst other features. It is interesting that the independent sector should pick up on alarms and technology so quickly, while social services have often been reluctant to see communication systems as part of care packages, frequently viewing them as part of housing and not personal care, as an emergency feature and not a communication system.

3. Homes can become more efficient with lower occupancy. Staff and bed resources are freed up and services such as short stay care, respite, luncheon clubs, bathing facilities, and day care may be offered.

4. If carers and relatives have had previous contact with a home they may be able to make a more informed choice should the need for residential care arise.

We can summarise this situation by illustrating factors pushing purchasers and providers toward diversification and those pulling them from what might be on offer in the future.

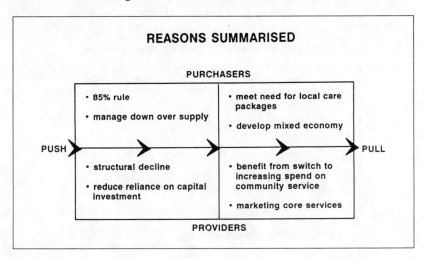

Not all factors will apply in any locality. For example, purchasers may be able to exercise choices in their community care strategies and diversification may not be a part of it. Other routes to a mixed economy include:

- developing existing organisations such as nursing or domiciliary care agencies,
- introducing new agencies into a locality,
- buying from NHS Trusts,
- creating community care Trusts.

These will very much depend on what their Community Care Plan tells them about:

- needs in their locality,
- the local supply situation,
- their philosophy about the merits or otherwise of small local providers and what users and carers are telling them about needs and the types of services required.

One very important dynamic that should be included in any local strategy is the capacity of providers to withstand changes in the community care market and their ability to respond. I call this a vulnerability matrix.

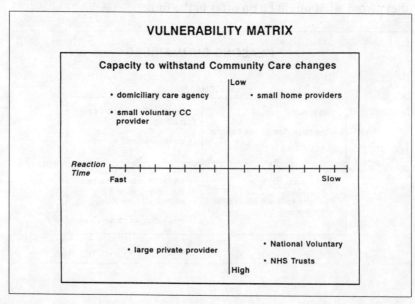

VULNERABILITY MATRIX

Capacity to withstand Community Care changes

Low

• domiciliary care agency   • small home providers

• small voluntary CC provider

Reaction Time

Fast   Slow

• large private provider   • National Voluntary

                                    • NHS Trusts

High

From a purchasing perspective there will be a range of types of providers and hence a variety of possible strategies to care for people at home. Our work suggests that many smal ..ʋme providers are highly vulnerable to the changes in community care assessment and financial regimes and thereby least well placed to respond to the changing environment.

The SSI Study

We were commissioned by the Social Services Inspectorate to review diversification possibilities and assist homes which might wish to diversify. We sought examples of good practice on a national basis and looked at diversification processes by concentrating our attention on five authorities across the country where on *a priori* grounds – over supply versus demand – diversification could be on purchaser and provider agendas. Fieldwork took place in February and March 1993 and focused on care for older people and people with a learning disability.

The major findings, and this is not surprising, is that residential care home providers can only diversify if there is a marketplace i.e. a purchaser for their services. As the domiciliary care agency business already knows, the private payers' market in the UK is considerably restricted. This means that unless contracts for diversified services are on offer the providers cannot respond.

Without this degree of strategic support, providers or their funders, such as banks and venture capital houses, do not have incentives for, or cannot contain the risks involved in, investment. They certainly need to be geared up to overcome the very practical barriers to diversification associated with VAT, insurance, costing and pricing services, new management skills and the diversification in thinking required to move into what are different industries.

On the purchaser side we found:

- residential care contract domination;
- underdevelopment of care package specifications combined with a lack of information on service design principles;
- insufficient detailed information in Community Care Plans and a lack of strategic purchasing plans or market analysis, and;

- a preference for developing existing domiciliary care providers or introducing new players into a locality rather than assisting homes to carry on caring.

On the provider side we found:

- an inability to plan their business or react to changed market circumstances (the stunned rabbit syndrome, caught in the glare of 1 April 1993);

- mis- and pre-conceptions about the meaning of day services, day care, domiciliary care and other diversified services; and

- a lack of information about purchasing intentions or the type and content of service they might commission.

For business enhancers – Chambers of Commerce, Enterprise Agencies, Economic Development Units – there was only a slow realisation that community care was undergoing major changes. We were particularly concerned that Economic Development Units, for example, do not appreciate the scale of the care home industry in their locality or the sorts of risks that were posed to employment by the community care changes. There is a clear need for social services and Economic Development Units to exchange information and work together.

Our conclusions are summarised in a series of messages to the major players. To purchasers the messages are:

1   Be clear and specific about service gaps – or when you can tell providers if not known.

- information is a vital resource in assisting providers to diversify;

- be open about your timetable for disclosure even if you do not know in detail what you will say at present;

- publish the steps you will take and the information you will collect to be able to make service gap data available;

- seek to analyse and manage the market – if there are no gaps say so.

2   Develop and share service design principles with the independent sector.

- as a precursor to devloping service specifications set the principles and values that you would expect to underlie day, domiciliary and respite care;

- build up pictures of the types of user you would want cared for – dependency, needs, care packages. Providers have lots of preconceptions and fantasies about what you might ask for and what they currently provide and how it might fit;

- take a current public service – for example, home help and home care and break it down into its constituent parts – showing what elements might be purchased. This will allow diversifiers to identify which elements of a package of care they might be able to contribute.

3   Publish service specifications.

- move on from residential and nursing home care and begin to develop new specifications for care packages and their components;

- share intended outcomes as part of that process and see what providers can innovate and offer to produce the intended impact for users and carers.

4   Resource diversification.

- where appropriate top-slice the STG or surplus or re-direct main programmes to offer real potential for would-be tenderers – some localities are diversifying their supply by holding back between 10-20 per cent of STG for this purpose;

- use the infrastructure money and/or joint finance as venture capital to defray development costs.

5   Move closer to selected suppliers.

- in some areas of under-provision a partnership approach to contracting and service development can work best;

- successful diversification probably works best where the purchaser understands and can support the business intentions of the provider;

- successful purchasing means building a new organisational structure to support suppliers inside the local authority and beyond it.

6   *Promote pilots, monitor and develop.*

- diversification is new but can be shown to work;

- purchasers should analyse the market and identify small-scale schemes that can be promoted and published;

- work with the trade associations and other business enhancers to disseminate these models;

- link up with your Economic Development Unit to ensure they are fully aware of the changes in community care and areas they might be involved in.

To providers the messages are:

1   *Not all can or should diversify.*

- diversification requires a critical mass of asset, management support and staffing;

- managerial capacity and competence is crucial. If your business is failing for lack of them now, diversification may not be for you;

- look at your competitors and listen to what your purchasers want. If the former are all diversifying you may need to be different. If you don't respond to the latter you could go under;

- geography and proximity to other homes and your customers are crucial variables – too many of the former and too few of the latter can cause problems.

2   *Diversifying services means diversifying your thinking.*

- running a care or nursing home business has probably meant being single-minded about getting started;

- starting to diversify means taking your existing business to pieces, looking at the parts critically and seeing how it can be repackaged;

- crucially, you have to look outside your business horizon to spot new needs and different requirements;

- you must analyse your market and your business – not just one or the other as in the past. The market is changing and so must your business.

3   Diversification is risky – assess other options as well.

- to be successful also means looking at your cost base – can it be reduced, made more efficient or quality improvements made?

- mergers may be less risky than committing resources to diversification;

- ensure the care for existing residents is sustained and improved wherever possible.

4   Seek support and assistance.

- approach your local TEC to gain access to business planning, master classes run on specific topics and other business support services;

- contact your local purchaser and explain your ideas and explore new diversification possibilities;

- know your way around your social services;

- work with care managers, care planners and contract managers.

Overall, we believe defensive diversification is difficult. Many homes have already diversified and only a small proportion will meet the overall test of fully replacing home income from diversified services.

The biggest single success factor for providers is the intention of the purchasers to contract for off-site or diversified services.

Thoughts for the future.
We are now clearly in a transitional phase between traditional and reformed community care systems. Funding is being transferred via STG to SSA. This should result in supply-led planning giving way to needs-led planning, in institutional care giving way to community care

public sector service base giving way to a mixed economy of

Diversification from residential and nursing home care is also in my opinion a transitional process. I believe that at the end of this transitional process (of around three years) we will not be talking about diversification but about some of the following features.

Consolidation

There will be, I believe, less fragmentation in both residential and domiciliary care sectors. This is already beginning to happen with corporate providers expanding their market share and their future capital investments. Whilst this creates some stability in supply, purchasers will need to exercise caution to ensure the homeliness of provision as outlined in *Caring for People* and to ensure local choices.

In the domiciliary sector consolidation of 'volume providers' is needed, and probably more so than in the residential sector. There needs to be consolidation to develop 'volume providers'. In turn this depends on significant contracts of a cost and volume, or block, nature being on offer to cover initial overheads and create confidence amongst suppliers and funders. A significant domiciliary care market cannot be created out of spot contracting.

A move beyond social security prices

It is important to pay for quality. It is recognised that good quality homely care costs more in residential care than social security levels permit. Local authority purchasers should move gradually away from reliance upon the benchmark of social security and into their own purchasing framework, dependent upon supply and quality. The care gap and the top-up costs for relatives suggest that social security level financing remains a problem.

However, other problems arise and in particular the emergence of a perverse incentive where maintaining residential care at DSS levels makes community care packages appear overly expensive. At present there is both purchaser and consumer resistance to paying for fully costed and priced non-residential services. This is partly historical, for local authorities have not always charged or indeed known the cost of their own care, and partly because there has been a reliance in the past upon the uncosted informal care of relatives, neighbours, friends.

When formal care substitutes for informal care the overall cost can come as a shock.

I do not believe it is possible to retain a rigorous charging framework within the residential care sector and not introduce a symmetrical version in the non-residential care sector. It is a question of local judgement as to whether there is a positive incentive for non-residential care or a perverse incentive where residential care is enforced.

Small local providers

Again a plea for purchasers to think carefully about quality as well as price in diversified community care services. There are already major volume providers in the home help service and potentially from NHS Trusts providing social care. Diversified providers in residential and nursing home care already have a stake in caring locally and can provide a source of responsive local services. They may cost more but that is a feature of the market if small local players are to be valued.

Ten years ago I undertook research into joint approaches in social policy, in particular looking at relations between the statutory and voluntary sectors. In this work I highlighted how local authorities gained the voluntary sector that they deserved. In other words, if a distant, difficult and uninventive voluntary sector was required, then do not resource the infrastructure of the voluntary sector. Some of the same may now be apparent between social services and the for-profit small scale sector.

References

KPMG Peat Marwick, *Diversification and the Independent Residential Care Sector,* Social Services Inspectorate, HMSO, 1993

Leat, D., *The Development of Community Care by the Independent Sector,* Policy Studies Institute, 1993

Whittingham, P., 'Diversity in Adversity', *Community Care,* 18 November 1993

Stimulating the Independent Sector in Rural Settings: Think Local – Think Small

Les Bright
Resources Development Manager,
Cambridgeshire Social Services Department

Cambridgeshire's project is concerned with developing new services for all client groups across the whole county. The county has a vast acreage of rich agricultural land with many small and isolated settlements, presenting us with markedly different challenges than those we were facing in the towns and cities where existing services were largely clustered. In this paper I will

- describe some of the specific rural issues;

- outline the approach adopted by our project;

- highlight the outcomes of that work;

- promote discussion on the range of approaches being adopted to stimulate provision in rural areas.

Rural issues
What follows is neither the most comprehensive nor detailed description of specific rural issues but is produced as a reminder of the kinds of factors affecting service users and those seeking to make provisions. These factors include:

- small(er) numbers of service users/would-be users/carers

- large(r) numbers of locations

- low(er) expectations of levels and types of provision

- great(er) distance from existing services

- absence of accessible transport or any transport at all

- high(er) costs of providing services because of travel costs or travelling time and limited opportunity to make economies of scale

- absence of kinship networks as a consequence of (a) younger people moving to towns for work/housing, and (b) older people moving to the countryside at or near the end of working lives

- under-development of the voluntary sector with many or most voluntary organisations located in towns or cities, mirroring public sector provision.

Cambridgeshire's approach

Any description of how the project has operated needs to begin with an outline of how the social services department is currently structured. More than five years ago the decision was taken to localise service provision. As a consequence 19 area teams were created to provide an integrated field/domiciliary/day/residential service to the public living within geographical patches. Area managers were encouraged to see themselves as having a stake in their patch to the extent of becoming actively involved in community affairs and voluntary organisations in particular.

Cambridgeshire would lay claim to having been an 'enabling authority' ahead of any legislative requirement: the vibrant grant aid programme supporting a diverse collection of voluntary organisations is evidence of this. Links with the private sector, or more specifically private care home proprietors, predate the project, with regular meetings to discuss matters of common interest being a feature of the last three or four years.

Partnership has not been an abstract concept. A wide range of new initiatives have been supported by the social services department through the commitment of resources in the form of either capital or revenue costs or staff time. So, on paper at least, 'ideal' conditions existed to stimulate new developments.

While our project was concerned with service development generally, an early decision was made that we should stimulate more domiciliary care services. Our first step was to undertake a *mapping exercise* to establish how many providers existed, what they were providing, and where they were located. That piece of work was interesting and helpful to us: interesting, because it revealed significantly more providers than any previous guesswork had suggested, and helpful, in terms of highlighting areas of need and types of service required.

The mapping exercise involved several strategies. We asked local authority staff about the providers they had used (frequently these were organisations approached at short notice to provide emergency cover); we contacted organisations which appeared in Yellow Pages, and we talked to people in organisations such as Crossroads and Age Concern. Having collected the information we then published it – within the department – so that it might be used by staff involved in arranging care packages. We encouraged those users (our staff) to give us feedback on the usefulness, accuracy and comprehensiveness of the directory, with the result that the next edition contained additional information.

But this activity did not of itself stimulate the independent sector; rather, it gave us a clue as to the kinds of things we should be encouraging to develop, and led us directly into the networking part of our strategy.

Networking – telling people and organisations what we were doing or what we wanted to do. We published a leaflet about the project and mailed it to:

- all existing recipients of grant aid;
- all registered residential/nursing care homes;
- coordinating bodies such as Councils of Churches, Rural Community Councils, Councils for Voluntary Service.

In addition we attended meetings of consultative fora established to work with voluntary organisations and private providers. Area managers and other interested staff were encouraged to inform their contacts such as local churches or parish councils.

What were we offering? The *promise* of some staff time to discuss ideas, or assistance in working them up; and the *threat* of cash either to pave the way for service development or to underwrite the cost of trying out an idea.

At a time when cash has become increasingly difficult to get hold of, in particular for new and untried approaches, there was a degree of disbelief about what we were offering. Voluntary organisations whose main grant aid has been reduced, or not adequately inflation-proofed, were sceptical about the value of short-term non-mainstream money.

Many private residential care providers were circumspect about responding to the challenge to diversify their business when their core activities were less stable than they had been for the preceding decade.

The outcomes

Given the responses of the voluntary and private sectors highlighted above, what has been the response, in particular for rural communities? Preliminary – sometimes terminal – discussions have been held with a very large number of individuals and organisations. Many of the smaller, village-based old people's day centres have seen the project as a way of providing additional grant aid to augment existing (inadequate) levels of funding, and others have been interested if project staff can deliver block contracts.

But networks work in ways that cannot always be predicted and project staff have provided advice, guidance and assistance to a significant number of sole traders and partnerships interested in gaining support for their ideas or emerging services.

A number of one and two person businesses, invariably focused on small communities, have received start-up help. Start-up help has enabled businesses to receive assistance in clarifying the shape, style and focus of the business and has bought guidance on routine matters connected with operating a business, such as insurance, dealing with the Inland Revenue, and designing publicity material. Small enterprises have received cash to meet the cost of publicity materials, to cover the costs of insuring the business and to meet the costs of travel or telephone. The businesses receiving start-up help are frequently aiming to serve the small communities previously ill-served by the public sector for the reasons outlined above.

The project has also provided financial support to enable potential/ actual providers to undertake market research aimed at identifying both the unmet needs of users and carers, and also the costs and problems encountered in establishing the business, such as how much purchasers (corporate and individual) will pay for the service – a critical issue in delivering services to a scattered customer base.

Have we done anything different? As well as building on our own existing organisational culture, we have been able to do something different: we have taken the risks and invested in infrastructure. Thinking small – and encouraging others to do so – has enabled us to meet customer needs in a bespoke fashion. Focusing on needs in this way, rather than on services, has been easier partly because there are few or no resources. It is too early to say how successful our approach has been but we will be monitoring our own progress closely.

*   *   *

DISCUSSION

It was agreed that stimulating the independent sector in rural areas raises many different issues from those associated with urban areas. Not only are there fewer providers who may be dispersed over a large area but there are likely to be fewer users with disparate needs.

Discussion centred on the need to adapt approaches to stimulating the independent sector to the resources that are available locally. For example, local organisations, such as parish councils, can be used as the base for service developments. Such an approach can lead to community ownership of new services and may help to engage other potential providers with future developments. Initially service developments should be focused on small scale and uncomplicated services, such as a lunch club, which will be easier to establish in the short term. More complicated services can be developed once a base has been established.

Because of the historic under-resourcing of many rural areas it seemed particularly relevant to encourage the development of new models of service provision. For example, different models of respite day care may be more appropriate in these areas than traditional models. However, it was acknowledged that existing providers might not recognise the need to change their services, nor have the time and finances to undertake the process.

Participants at the seminar raised the concern that issues regarding community care are often low down on a rural community's list of priorities. For example, transport, housing and crime are often thought to be of more pressing concern than the community care needs of a minority of the population. There may be a tension between those who plan service developments and the wishes of the community. These tensions need to be addressed if a partnership approach is to be established; otherwise communities may become ambivalent about any new service developed.

Ensuring Quality at Arm's Length

David Dobson
Project Officer for *Caring for People who Live at Home* Initiative,
North Yorkshire Social Services Department

Background

The pursuit of a set of quality standards and accompanying systems
for providers of care at home is one of the four strands of the North
Yorkshire *Caring for People who Live at Home* Initiative. The other
three activities are:

Market analysis

York Health Economics Consortium and the Social Policy Research
Unit of the University of York completed a major piece of research
and market analysis in July 1993, the principal aims of which were to:

- understand the current supply of non-residential provision in the
  independent sector;

- understand current and likely future demands for such provision;

- identify the potential for the development of non-residential
  provision in the independent sector.

The target groups for the market analysis and for the Initiative as
a whole are older people and adults with a range of mental health
problems, physical disabilities and learning disabilities. The target
services are home care, meals, day services, respite care and other
types of domiciliary care.

43

Business development counselling

The Department has been working jointly with the County Council's Economic Development Centre to fulfil that part of the project that promotes the development of new businesses, not-for-profit organisations and the diversification of current providers' services.

The proposed model is based on the small business adviser approach adopted for other types of businesses. It was recognised in the market analysis that small and medium sized organisations in the private and voluntary sector need access to sound business counselling advice, rather than information covering social care issues. The York University market analysis identified over 100 initial expressions of interest in the development of new services to people living at home.

Through the funds allocated to the project, three business counsellors have been commissioned to run seminars for independent providers, to be followed up by individual counselling sessions with a number of agencies.

Funding for projects

The funds available to promote activity in the voluntary and private sector are an important component of the Initiative. North Yorkshire has earmarked money for two kinds of funding, both of which are conditional on the viability of any project to attract permanent and future funding from statutory or private sources. The two types of funding are small one-off grants and pump-priming funding.

- *small, one-off grants:* these are one-off grants given for the purpose of extending a current independent sector service or to set up new independent sector services which will increase service users' choice; and

- *pump-priming projects:* these are funds given to an independent sector provider for a maximum of two years for schemes which extend users' choice in priority areas. Projects given financial support in this way act as model/demonstration projects with longer-term relevance.

Quality standards for the home care industry

The fourth activity relates to quality standards. In the absence of any national registration/inspection guidelines (unlike those which exist in the residential sector) how do social services departments and the home care industry come up with appropriate quality standards for home care services for people living in their own homes?

In North Yorkshire, following a series of meetings with the independent sector, a group of 20 people – a mix of independent care agencies and social services staff – are now working in five groups to develop:

(a) a North Yorkshire Home Care Standards Council to promote quality standards in domiciliary care;

(b) a Home Care Users' Charter;

(c) training for home care providers;

(d) knowledge and expertise on insurance issues relating to independent sector home care agencies;

(e) a set of quality standards to which home care agencies should subscribe.

This work is not being carried out in isolation and/or without access to available source material. In the initial stages, we have been guided by the work of Lesley Bell of the Joint Advisory Group Domiciliary Care Association; the work of the United Kingdom Home Care Association; and the work going on in some of the other 14 local authorities which are part of the *Caring for People who Live at Home* Initiative.

One of the early lessons learned from the York University market analysis and research was the importance of a shared understanding between agencies; 'adversarial' contracting is unlikely to provide quality or continuity of service for users.

The North Yorkshire approach to ensuring quality

1. Wherever possible work positively and openly with independent sector providers on home care issues.

2. Keep the independent sector informed of current developments through:

   – regular bulletins/briefings;

   – local seminars;

   – personal contact.

3. Wherever possible, liaise with users/carers.

4. Make use of up-to-date thinking and publications from people involved in similar activities.

In North Yorkshire, we are attempting to create a 'Kitemark' to which home care agencies, including social services, will subscribe. The 'Kitemark' will be supported by a County Home Care Standards Council which will ensure that standards are adhered to.

Quality definitions

The simple definitions we are using are as follows:

- *Quality* is providing services that meet standards based on customers' needs as efficiently as possible every time;

- *Quality assurance* is a system which ensures that the customers always get what they have been promised;

- *Quality control* is a system of checking/testing/inspecting a service to ensure that standards and targets have been met.

Conclusion

We aim to implement the major part of the Quality Standards Initiative by the end of April 1994. The commitment and enthusiasm that has been expressed by those independent sector representatives who are working with social services staff suggests that the Quality Standards Initiative will have positive outcomes.

*   *   *

DISCUSSION

The seminar presentation prompted a general discussion on the need to ensure that all providers of domiciliary and day care within the independent and statutory sectors were providing good quality services. It was generally agreed that some form of 'quality standards' are necessary to ensure that the social care market is not swamped by 'fly-by-night' operators who are difficult to regulate. However, the means by which such regulation is achieved were keenly debated.

Discussion focused on whether or not quality standards should be established through national registration, local voluntary accreditation, by individual providers or by a provider representative body. All approaches to this issue will have repercussions for the emergent market. For example, a proliferation of local authorities developing their own accreditation systems may inhibit those providers from developing services that operate across boundaries. On the other hand, whilst the development of a national registration scheme may lead to consistent standards being adopted across the market, they may place onerous burdens on small organisations and inhibit their development.

The general perception of the workshop was that some form of assurance of the quality of day and domiciliary services was essential. However, a general concern was raised that whatever form of quality standards is adopted they should not be seen as minimum requirements to enter the market. Purchasers and providers should be encouraged to work together in the pursuit of excellence and the satisfaction of the user should be the main focus of this partnership.

Business Planning

Mike Morris
Development Worker, Social Care Enterprise Agency, Shropshire

The Social Care Enterprise Agency was planned as part of Shropshire's commitment to Care in the Community. The Agency was set up at arm's length from the social services department and is housed in its own premises. It comprises a small team of people with business skills who had previously worked in public and private sector consultancy.

The role of the Agency is to develop partnerships between local authority provision and independent sector provision. A major part of the Agency's work is to provide business planning advice to independent operators who wish to offer a community care service. The Agency works alongside the social services department assessing independent sector service proposals and providing business guidance on service development.

This paper will explore some of the practical problems and complexities of stimulating the provision of community care services by the independent sector. It will draw on our work in Shropshire and highlight the relevance of our experience for others involved in planning community care businesses. I propose to do this by examining an actual case study which has required a great deal of planning effort over the last few months. Before doing this however, I would like to outline some of the principles of business planning which underlie our work.

Allen Hickling (1974) highlights the four basic trade-offs which make up the key characteristics of decision making, namely:

- *Simplification versus the recognition of complexity.* Building even the most basic planning model is quite a complex task. We need to simplify where possible without losing validity.

- *Urgency versus diligence.* We have all been here! There is always pressure to make quick decisions but you have to hold on to the need for relevant information to enable you to make an informed choice.

- *The balance of commitment versus flexibility* Being committed to clear goals is vital whilst still managing to keep as many options open as possible.

- *The problems of incrementality versus comprehensiveness* Incrementality is sometimes described as the art of muddling through but many problems are not easily solved in one go. Some decisions have to be reached in a piecemeal fashion. Some may have to be deferred.

Each of these four basic trade-offs is normally present in the business planning process, and they encapsulate the difficulties most of us will experience in either preparing or evaluating 'real' cases.

The Shropshire Social Care Enterprise Agency has developed a checklist to help with the assessment of social care business plans. It includes the following factors – in no particular order:

- the complexity of the project;
- the existing skills of the staff and their future skill needs;
- the funding – initial and ongoing – which is available;
- the detail and accuracy of data and information;
- the optimism and sensitivity of income projections;
- the bases for, and sensitivity of, cost projections;
- the time-frame of the investment and the payback period, if required.

The techniques for evaluating these factors range from the subjectively simple to the objectively complex. In the next section I want to use a case study to show how the evaluation of businesses becomes more difficult in practice.

The case study

Broseley Cottage Hospital was built at the turn of the century in a small community of some 5,000 people. The immediate surrounding area takes that figure up to around 30,000. The hospital was closed in 1989 in the face of strong local opposition. Before closure a group of local people negotiated with the district and regional health authorities and were eventually granted a 99-year lease at a peppercorn rent. The health authority also commissioned and paid for a report by Peat Marwick McLintock who recommended that the site could be developed for a small – 25 bedded – nursing home. The trustees planned to sell part of the site to a developer for housing and use the income from the sale to open the new nursing home.

Negotiations were about to be concluded when the developer went out of business. The trustees then had to re-market the site and eventually two housing associations showed an interest. By this time it had become apparent that the market for nursing home care was not likely to materialise. The trustees prepared a new proposal based upon a reduced number of nursing beds but with the addition of a day care facility. Planning permission for this new proposal was sought from the local district council for Section 106 approval and a request made to the Health Authority for a change of use under the terms of the lease.

The Social Care Enterprise Agency became involved in this scheme in August 1993 when a detailed business plan was required for the new proposal. Given the short period of time with which the trustees had to work, the Agency offered assistance with the preparation of the business plan. Since this had become a time-led assignment, the Agency began by dividing the remaining time into three clear stages.

Stage 1

The first six weeks were allocated to an assessment of the available options. Having identified the strongest options the Agency prepared an outline business plan for discussion with the trustees. This work was scheduled to be completed by 30 September 1993.

Stage 2

Having presented our outline plans to the trustees we allocated four weeks to finalising the submission to the district council. This process involved the selection of the preferred option, and carrying out modifications and refinements. The deadline for this work was 31 October.

Stage 3

In the final stage the Agency liaised between the trustees, the health authority, the district council, their respective lawyers and representatives, and other interested parties. Contracts were to be exchanged on 17 December 1993.

The Agency examined the implications of each of the options in relation to market and demand considerations, the operating costs and income to be generated, and the capital funding and development required. For each option the Agency isolated the 'High Definition Problem Areas' which needed to be addressed.

Not all of the questions raised during this process required immediate solutions. McNees and Perna (1982), in an article on an eclectic approach to forecasting variables, urge planners to use every bit of information, external and internal, which is available to them. They encourage planners to take a 'personal view' on where the economy, central and local government policy, inflation, taxation, etc, is heading. The Agency, in adopting a 'personal view' of the community care context, became aware of how quickly health and social care policy had changed in the last four years.

Hickling (1974) says planning is a non linear, cyclical process where 'thoughts need to be recycled and where much of the planning process is incremental'. In other words, going around in circles can be a very productive exercise.

The outcome

In our case we went around the circle a number of times. We identified three different functions for which the Cottage Hospital could be used. We examined four different levels of potential activity/demand and we assessed several alternative complementary capital development plans. Underpinning all our activity was a desire to balance flexibility and commitment whilst recognising, and holding on to, the wishes of the community we were trying to assist. In some of our models, our answers 'proved' that a particular outcome was not viable.

One of our main roles in the development planning process was to offer responsible advice. In order to do this effectively, from the outset we had to be honest about our limitations: time and again we have seen apparently insurmountable barriers swept aside in the face of strong local commitment.

On 30 September we met with the trustees and recommended that the Broseley Cottage Hospital should be developed into a Day Care Centre offering day care seven days a week. Our planning showed that there was a local demand for day care. We allowed for a slow build-up of usage, partly to mirror the natural demand growth, but also to allow for the development of staff and their accompanying infrastructure. The business plan showed that, whilst there would be a manageable shortfall in the first operating year, this would be followed by break-even position in the second, and a surplus by the third year.

The business plan we put forward to the trustees was accepted in principle. It was re-worked and refined to reflect their comments. At the same time more detailed architectural plans were drawn up and preliminary development costs confirmed.

On 31 October a detailed business plan was presented by the trustees and the Agency to the health authority and the district council. The business plan was agreed on 12 November. The five groups of lawyers representing the interests of the trustees, the district council, two housing associations and the health authority are currently attempting to exchange contracts by 17 December 1993. The planned opening date for the Cottage Hospital Day Care Centre is now set at April 1995. The Enterprise Agency is now working alongside two other Cottage Hospital trustee groups who are planning similar developments.

We do not present this case study as a paradigm of business planning. There is no single 'right' or 'wrong' approach, but rather 'shades of suitability' which may draw upon one or more of techniques ranging from the relatively simple, such as the 'If then, what?' analysis to sophisticated operational research methods.

In attempting to apply business planning to community care there are a number of questions concerning skills and training, duties, responsibilities, confidentiality and conflicting interests which need to be addressed, but have not been discussed in this paper.

In summary, business planning:

• provides a model for evaluating the project which, whilst not an absolute guarantee of success, will alert you to predictable causes of failure;

- provides a means of monitoring progress;

- enables the resources which will be needed to be identified, and tells you when you will need them;

- provides the opportunity to identify problems in advance, and;

- provides the basis for a continuous and critical process through the life of a project.

In Shropshire we are encouraging the application of business planning skills in a number of areas and to a number of schemes. As part of the *Caring for People who Live at Home* Initiative we are monitoring our own progress – both the successes and the difficulties.

*   *   *

DISCUSSION

A large part of the discussion was about the practicalities of formulating business plans and the associated business culture. Firstly, the length of time and costs involved in producing a business plan were addressed. In the example given in the workshop presentation, of Broseley Cottage Hospital, a total of four weeks had been taken to produce a business plan for a project scale of £200,000. It was suggested that the process might be shorter for smaller-scale projects, and that costs vary according to whether or not a consultant has to be brought in to develop the plan. An estimate of £250-300 per day was estimated for private consultants.

The competence of local authorities to operate within the business planning culture was brought into question. The view given by the presenter was that the business culture is here to stay and that social services departments will have to learn how to operate within it for the sake of their own businesses and services. Concern was also expressed about the capacity of small providers, such as self-employed individuals and small worker cooperatives, to operate within this culture. In response to this, it was suggested that very simple business plans can be developed for small businesses and that it is not necessary to use over-complicated business planning in this area.

Another issue raised for discussion was charging policies, with independent providers expressing concern that they are obliged to cover all their costs whereas social services departments are not. However, it was said that all sectors are concerned about the need for a 'level playing field' and each believes the slope to be against them. In addition it was pointed out that local authorities are going to have to put unit costs for their own services into their community care plans in the future. This may assist the independent sector in developing and/or improving their business plans.

References

Hickling, A., *Managing Decisions: The Strategic Choice Appeal,* Mantec Publications, 1974

McNees, S. and Perna, N., 'Forecasting Macroeconomic Variables – An Eclectic Approach' in McKridakis and Wheelwright, *The Handbook of Forecasting – A Manager's Guide,* John Wiley & Sons, 1982

Buying the Best?

Heather Stephens
Principal Officer, Community Care Planning,
Barnsley Social Services Department

Contracting for care with the independent sector

This paper will examine the way in which Barnsley Metropolitan Borough Council have worked in partnership with voluntary sector providers to develop a wider range of high quality domiciliary and day care services. The contract culture has grown at a considerable pace since the mid-1980s. Most departments within the local authority have adopted the approach, either by choice or coercion, although social services departments have been slower than many – more so in some areas where there is a conflict of ideology between the political persuasion of local and national government.

One reason for social services being slower to commit themselves to a contract culture is that they have not had the legislative requirements of Compulsory Competitive Tendering (CCT) and market testing present in other areas of the public sector. However, the introduction of the purchaser/provider split in the Griffiths Report translated into the requirements of the NHS and Community Care Act and the more generalist Citizen's Charter, have persuaded many departments of the wide range of benefits resulting from this approach. Benefits such as choice, consumer control, needs-led services, increased accountability, better quality and competition leading to better value for money.

This is the setting against which the Barnsley Metropolitan Borough Council embarked upon the *Caring for People who Live at Home* Initiative. For an authority which is rightly proud of its direct provider and good employer record, it is something of a milestone to embrace an Initiative the objective of which is to stimulate domiciliary and day care developments in the independent sector. Barnsley is committed to ensuring better outcomes for service users, particularly in enabling people to remain in their own homes. It has been recognised that additional funding for in-house developments is not going to be available and the only way in which services are to be extended in level and type is through stimulating independent sector development. The 85 per cent of the Special Transitional Grant to be spent on the independent sector has offered an opportunity to establish community care services to provide a choice of agency, type and level of domiciliary and day care services.

Given that we are going to contract for these services from the independent sector, a number of issues have had to be addressed, not least so that we would end up buying the best we could within the resources available.

Our first question had to be: 'What is our purchasing strategy?' In considering this we had to decide whether we were going to commission services which would complement our own services or those which would also compete with the directly provided services. If we were to take seriously the issue of expanding choice to the consumer we, at least, had to begin the process by acknowledging that in offering a wider range, level and type of service we would be commissioning services from independent agencies which could be viewed as competitors to our own.

In reality, the services offered by our own in-house providers will continue to be needed, with the independent sector offering complementary and supplementary services. In many cases care packages are being put together using a combination of both statutory and independent sector provision.

Our next question was: 'What services do we want to buy?' In determining this we identified:

- the *needs* for specific client groups, and which elements of those needs we were going to address as a matter of priority;

- the *current services* available, in relation to location, agency, type and level. From this we were then able to identify what *gaps/deficits* there were.

We then used this information to identify our *Community Care Strategy* i.e. the services we were going to purchase to increase choice and the level and range of services.

Our next consideration was whether we bought from the statutory/ voluntary or private sector, from agencies/companies/ organisations or individuals.

In Barnsley we have a history of working on joint projects with voluntary agencies, particularly through grant aid schemes. As the first phase of our purchasing strategy for domiciliary and day care, it was decided to consider commissioning services from those voluntary agencies which had considerable expertise in providing services similar in nature to those we required, with services from the private sector being considered as part of phase two. Agencies, companies and organisations will form part of our purchasing strategy, but at this time there is no intention to contract with individuals directly for services, other than those individual homeowners who fall within the contract for residential or nursing care.

Our next concern was: 'What type of contract?'

- Should we use block contracts where a specified amount of service is bought in a block, with a price agreed in advance?

- Should we use cost/volume contracts where a specified amount of service to be available is determined to a minimum and maximum activity level at a cost determined in advance?

- Should we use spot purchase where the price is agreed at time of purchase by the budget holder in discussion with the provider?

  or

- Should we use call-off contracts where the price is agreed in advance or is a standard price determined by the authority?

Having agreed to commission specific services from the voluntary sector, block contracts were used. A set amount of money was to be given to each agency for a specified amount, type and level of service. It was, however, agreed at this time that, where a person's individual care package could not be fully implemented using services from the statutory and voluntary sector, private sector agencies could be used on a spot purchase basis. This was subject to approval by council committee. This arrangement has only been required in two instances in the past three months.

Although we decided to commission services from the voluntary sector we still needed to consider how we were going to stimulate a market response. Should we go out to *tender*, go through a process to identify a list of *select providers*, or advertise for *invitations of interest*?

Our aim at the beginning was to ensure that we ended up buying the best service for the money available. 'Best' in this case meant 'fitness for purpose', the purpose having been gleaned from information on needs, current service audit etc. Our main concern was that there were a number of changes in the way in which services were operating which might have an impact on that identified need. We did not know how changes in the social services department's home care and the introduction of new services, as well as the introduction of care management itself, were going to affect service need.

The agencies or organisations we wanted to contract with were those with which we would be able to work in partnership to build into the contract process flexibility and responsiveness to changes in need. We selected providers based on experience in the relevant field, our working relationship with them and general requests for interest in contracting with us. It was very much the 'tap on the shoulder' approach. In some instances we were approached by voluntary organisations with innovative ideas.

We emphasised the need for jointly negotiated specifications and contracts, with providers involved from the earliest possible stage. This has allowed us to build in an element of flexibility and responsiveness within the contract. Both partners, the social services department and the voluntary agency concerned, understand the need for a specification which may change over a period of time as the information on needs changes.

We are now moving toward developing a standard framework specification and contract which will enable us to enter into call off contracts, particularly with private sector providers. This framework will enable us to devise a list of approved suppliers and this, supported by individual client care contracts, will allow us to call off contracts as and when required.

If we are going to ensure that we are buying the best we have to be confident that *quality outcomes* are being achieved. By this we mean that the services *meet needs*, provide *choice*, go some way to developing the *mixed economy* and provide *value for money*.

This can be done via the *specification* which will include both quantifiable and qualitative outputs. At a future date *accreditation* may be available for some agencies, for example, a voluntary registration scheme for domiciliary care agencies.

Monitoring, both by the provider agency and the purchasing side will need to be frequent and regular – we are currently looking at small project teams undertaking this task. Most importantly, monitoring of outcomes would be incomplete without consumer involvement. The specification includes a requirement for *consumer satisfaction* measures to be undertaken at regular intervals. This together with a well publicised *complaints system* will help us to *review and modify* the service to ensure that we really are 'buying the best' from the consumer's point of view as well as our own.

* * *

DISCUSSION

There were concerns that local authorities might be unprepared to fund the services that they want from the voluntary organisations and that the pioneering aspect of voluntary organisations will be lost in the new contract culture. Some local authorities were said to find voluntary organisation more politically palatable than the private sector and were therefore more likely to do business with them. It was queried whether there was 'a level playing field'. Some voluntary organisations expressed concerns about being self-financing and getting into the contracting process.

Barnsley are building consumer satisfaction into their contracts. One of the independent providers said that consumer satisfaction was not a new concept but the issue was how to monitor it. The difficulty of quantifying consumer satisfaction was discussed and it was asked whether these indicators should be developed by the provider or the user.

The merits of block contracts as opposed to spot purchasing were discussed. It was asked whether providers should be involved in drawing up specifications. If providers were involved, the specifications might be more realistic. Purchasing intentions need to be explicitly stated so that providers have some idea of the size and type of services they are being asked to tender for. There was a discussion around GP fund-holders and their involvement in the contracting system in the future.

Stimulating the Independent Sector to Create and Deliver Services to African, Caribbean and Asian People

Josephine Kwhali
Assistant Director, Quality Assurance and Planning, London
Borough of Hammersmith and Fulham Social Services Department

Individuals and organisations involved in the process of developing specific services for black people have to ask themselves why such a necessity arises within a society that has long been multi-racial, multi-faith and multi-lingual. Given this historical and functional condition, mainstream services and the organisations which provide and fund them might be expected to meet need in a manner reflective of lived reality. Instead, black people are frequently marginalised to the sidelines as a discrete 'client group' and/or an interesting (and frequently problematic) source of study or – perhaps worse still – their specific needs and experiences ignored. Meanwhile, services continue to develop as if there were an ethnically cohesive society into which 'minorities' must be fitted or integrated, regardless of their wishes and needs.

The creation and delivery of services to black people cannot be viewed outside the framework of discrimination, ethnocentricism and racism, which insidiously prevents black people's needs being structurally addressed in a centralised way. Neither can principles of human justice be entirely ignored if social services believes itself to be a 'caring' profession. If we do so, then we fail to predict the issues, possibilities and tensions of 'black specific' developments and are in danger of perpetuating that which already exists, albeit clothed in a different way.

The beginnings of community care consultation in the London Borough of Hammersmith and Fulham clearly and directly communicated to the organisation what the majority of black staff (and some white staff too) already knew. The black community were no longer prepared to wait and suffer until a hypothetical construction of 'integrated' and 'pluralistic' services was developed. They had needs now and they wanted them met.

The African, Caribbean and Asian communities saw little evidence of 'integration' meaning anything more than them integrating into what already existed and then having to struggle for basic requirements such as appropriate food, health care, religious rights etc. If they were unable or unwilling to use 'mainstream' services they went without, were forced to 'look after their own' or made do with voluntary initiatives that were often poorly funded. They did not want this model reproduced for community care.

Black people, whether as users, carers, staff or managers, did not want 'special' services out of any desire for separatism. Black people are experts on the dangers and realities of such a concept. They simply wanted services that met their needs, and had little confidence that this could or would be speedily achieved unless those services emerged from the realities of their own existence, experiences and defined needs, and unless they were managed by black people themselves. They recognised that many people within the social services department were doing their best and trying to effect change, but felt that this was not going to resolve speedily the very real care needs that existed. They wanted services based on their own definitions of need, rather than the local authority controlling and defining black reality; they wanted to directly manage and control the services that emerged and they wanted basic human justice.

This was the challenge which the *Caring for People who Live at Home* Initiative presented to Hammersmith and Fulham. A number of key issues and principles informed the development of the project:

1. Consultation has to be extensive, detailed and genuine. There are no shortcuts.

2. It is not sufficient merely to consult the black leaders or established bodies such as the CRE, as their views and experiences may not be representative of black carers, users and people denied services or struggling to have their needs met in appropriate ways.

3. Consultation is particularly complex with black people who have seldom been systematically consulted on any fundamental aspect of British social policy or service delivery and may be disillusioned with agencies they perceive and experience as predominantly white and unconcerned with their specific needs. Simply because social services and health departments may now wish to consult with black people, you cannot assume that they will wish to talk to you! They may feel that black people's needs have been long discussed and identified but less seldom acted upon.

4. Black people are not a homogeneous 'blob'. The consultation process and the people undertaking it have to represent the racial, ethnic and linguistic diversity of the community and it must be done in ways sensitive to religious and cultural norms. There is little point in holding a consultation event on a religious festival day or sending along an English speaker if the prospective participants speak Urdu.

5. The issues and messages emerging from consultation may be painful and difficult for the organisation to hear. If you can't stand the heat then don't go near the fire! Similarly, if you are expecting praise and affirmation for the initiatives already undertaken (if indeed there have been any) then you may be in for a surprise, as black people may feel they have little for which to be grateful.

6. The people who know most about being black (whether African, Caribbean or Asian in origin) are those who are black. It is pointless to begin black focused initiatives unless the organisation starts from this premiss and recognises that the reality of lived experience must be the key determinant. To impose on to black people white people's analysis of black experience, reality and need is to further alienate black people from the organisational process.

7. If the organisation simply wishes black people to affirm what they have already decided to do (or not do) in the manner they have decided to do it, there is little point in consulting.

8. What emerges from the consultation may have little in common with the original concept. In its *Caring for People who Live at Home* submission, the social services department proposed an independent domiciliary care agency for African, Caribbean and

Asian People. We are now establishing two Community Care resource centres which will bring together day centre, luncheon club, carers, domiciliary care, volunteers and advice and information, as this is what consultation suggested people both needed and wanted.

A project designed to be of benefit to black people cannot legitimately be designed to meet organisational preferences if they do not accord with people in need and the views of those who know what it is to be black.

9. Black people embrace all the equality target groups. The consultation and outline project must therefore address issues of gender, disability and sexuality. To do otherwise is to continue to marginalise key groups and needy individuals and create divisions within the community itself.

10. Black framed initiatives require considerable time and support. The concept and the reality of specific services will need to be defended and argued for time and time again with those who actively seek to undermine such projects or simply do not understand why black people cannot use existing services and 'integrate'. Racism and racial understanding are complex and emotive concepts – if you are not prepared to grapple with their expression and have a considered strategy for so doing, there is little purpose in proceeding.

The process of meeting the community care needs of African, Caribbean and Asian people
Evaluation
What already exists and where are the gaps? Are these services discrete and specifically tailored to meet the racial, cultural, religious and linguistic experiences and needs of black people, or are black people 'fitted in' to mainstream, majority group provision?

Consultation
What do black users, carers and community members themselves want and how do we know that they will tell us? What methods of consultation are appropriate? How should it be undertaken and by whom, and who evaluates and decides upon the outcomes?

Deliberation
Carefully think through the results of evaluation and consultation and the implications of the existing organisational structures for what is possible, practical and achievable within the time and financial limitations.

Communication
Communicate with the black communities, staff, mangers, elected members and interested others. Developing discrete services for black people within the constraints of a white organisation is a contradiction in terms. Communication of intentions, concept, black people's needs and hoped for outcomes is a vital component.

Condemnation
Whilst black people's needs have seldom been adequately met within mainstream organisations and the challenge of services to a multi-racial clientele less than effectively addressed, discrete services for black people are frequently condemned, as are the people who promote them. The factors that restrict black people's access to appropriate mainstream services may well be in force when trying to develop provision appropriate to their needs. The reality of racism has to be acknowledged and strategically addressed if the Initiative is not to be undermined.

Marginalisation
The provision of discrete services for black people does not mean separatist service provision. A specific project simply extends choice. Mainstream services will continue to have an urgent and primary need to develop in a manner relevant to multi-racial Britain.

Action
Nothing will happen and nothing will develop unless you take informed and sustained action. A community care project for black people is *hard work* and has the potential for failure. However – non-action is in itself ACTION!

Evaluation
Evaluation should take place at every stage, by and with the black community who are the expected beneficiaries. In practical terms, the

department has begun to develop a Community Care resource centre for the Asian community and a similar initiative for the African-Caribbean community. These will serve several functions, including:

- luncheon club provision;

- day centre and social provision;

- an office base for carers' associations and meeting space for carers themselves;

- a base for volunteers;

- domiciliary care activity;

- information and advice about community care and health agency/social services;

- health education.

The Centres are being adapted and refitted to meet statutory (environmental health, EU, fire etc.) requirements and the local structural requirements of the communities. We wish the centres to reflect in their surroundings and decor the ethnic groups they will be servicing.

Many of the people expected to use the service will have complex needs and are likely to be cared for at home (or in the community) with packages of care. As such, some of the services will be directly commissioned through the main social and health service purchasing mechanisms. The centres will also be free to 'sell' their services to other agencies or to residents with lower level needs who would not qualify for services but who are willing to pay. The agencies will also be able to consider income generation from sponsorship, business etc.

A formal tendering process is currently being carried out to appoint an organisation to run and manage the resource centres. A clear service specification has been drawn up to cover both the discrete racial and ethnic service needs as well as the business and financial knowledge and expertise required to run a resource centre.

The whole process has been and continues to be demanding, time consuming and exhausting. Some of the process (i.e. building works) remain outside of social services' control. Many aspects take far longer to reach agreement and completion than could have been predicted, and competing interests, ideologies, power relationships and needs have to be reconciled and addressed. Many members of the target communities have reconciled themselves to 'making do' and find it hard to really believe something more might be possible. Sometimes mainstream staff can feel threatened and exhibit this in a lack of interest or support. Others may feel they are implicitly being criticised for not previously doing more to meet black need or are confused as to how they should proceed.

An innovatory project such as the one being established in Hammersmith and Fulham is not, however, about blame or self-recrimination. It simply begins from the reality of what actually is and proceeds on the basis that we want to change 'what is' to something different and appropriate to black people's community care needs. Ultimately, we hope that the service will be:

- Responsive
- Realistic
- Resourced
- Reflective

and, in those gloomy moments when the vision of what might be begins to fade – REAL.

*   *   *

DISCUSSION
Discussion focused on a number of issues arising from the aim of the project to develop services specifically for minority ethnic groups. Participants were interested in determining how this had been achieved, and in drawing out some of the difficulties they faced in their own authorities. It was acknowledged that the process had been, and is likely to be, political in both senses of the word. The need to define the reasons for such a service development very precisely was emphasised, as was the need to focus on a small number of specific goals rather than aiming for anything too ambitious. The presenter was also keen to point out that the process is likely to take a long time, and that it requires commitment from someone who has power within the social services department and the trust of the relevant local communities if the project is to succeed.

The development of integrated, as against segregated, services was discussed. The emphasis was placed on providing members of minority ethnic groups with choice, and on recognising that these communities have not been served well in the past. The view was expressed that integrated services should be developed alongside segregated services, since mainstream services would never otherwise address the needs of the whole community. The need to recognise diversity within minority ethnic communities was discussed, and emphasis was placed on comprehensive consultation. It was pointed out by the presenter that the services would not have developed in the way they had in Hammersmith and Fulham if left to the conventional service planning process. Finally, participants discussed equal opportunities policies, and the need to reflect the cultural and religious requirements of different communities within them, for example female carers to female clients for certain religious groups.

Concluding Remarks

Andrew Williamson
Director of Social Services, Devon County Council

In concluding today's programme, I want to share with you some thoughts and ideas about the development of services for users and carers. In my view, the combined legislative changes of recent years, when taken together with the enforced changes within the agencies with whom we deal, has led to the biggest single change in the provision of welfare sevices since the creation of the welfare state. Inevitably when you move from a service-led approach (Chart 1) to a

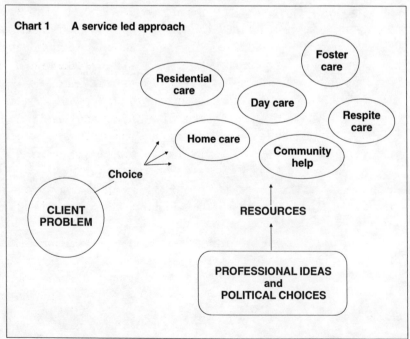

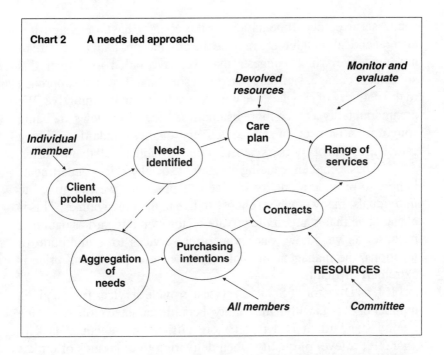

Chart 2   A needs led approach

needs-led approach (Chart 2), cultural change and, therefore, benefit to the user takes time to achieve. It is no surprise to me that Diana Leat made reference to a slow start in the involvement of users. Those of us who are responsible for the development or services in rural areas in this country, know that there is no magical formula for mobilising local communities, and that by definition 'these things take time'.

As we come to the end of the first year of community care, I believe we are on the verge of significant change in the delivery of services. Local purchasing must be the most exciting way forward. The notion that you can involve local people in making decisions about how their money should be spent and the order of priorities, goes to the roots of community development programmes. In my own authority, as we develop the skill of devolving power to local communities, there is a growing sense of anticipation at the implicit power contained within a local purchasing plan.

As I listen to some of the difficulties that Isobel Allen reported this morning, I have to say that as the director of a social services department, I am not surprised. The agenda for change which has been externally driven over the past four years, would, in my view have defeated many private sector organisations. As far as I am aware, social services departments across the country have delivered this agenda and, although there may be the odd hiccup, I am not aware of any evidence which suggests that we have failed to deliver this significant change. I am sure that given some stability in our approach to the delivery of services, we will learn a lot from this Initiative. We are undoubtedly a much more listening service. User views are being sought for all aspects of service delivery, quality standards are being established and of course we are required to publicise all that we offer.

The basic challenge facing the staff of social services departments is how to provide a quality service at a price that we can afford to individuals, many of whom choose to live in their own homes. This is a challenge that many in the private sector would regard as daunting because, as we know, once you offer services to a multitude of locations, the management challenge to ensure quality and price is extremely difficult.

If I, as Director of Social Services, provide services from a given number of outlets within the county, I could guarantee more easily the quality standard. It is a much more difficult management task to guarantee a level of quality when delivering to thousands of outlets that one does not control. I would contend at the present time that it is too early to review success or failure of this Initiative as many of our predictions span a two to three year timescale. We know there are too many private sector residential beds in some parts of the country and not enough private sector involvement in other parts. This will not change overnight. Our experience within Devon is that across the range of services provided we are seeing improvements. That is not to deny that some members of staff are very unhappy about the extent of the paperwork involved. It is worth remembering that in taking responsibility for funding the private residential sector from the Department of Social Security, we also assumed responsibility for the administration of this multi-million pound system.

We now know much more about the existing market. District managers are expected to know about all forms of service provision within their boundaries and to be aware of the quality provided. We are learning about contracting and forecasting. We are listening to users and carers. Many of us have established forums where providers of services from all sectors meet with the users of services, and we are becoming increasingly skilful at putting together imaginative packages of care.

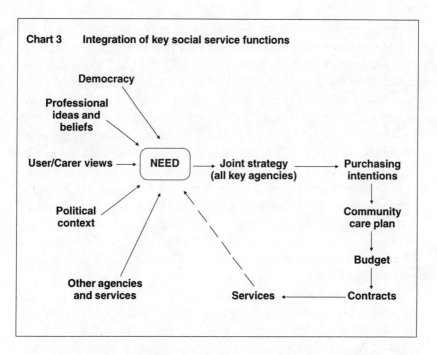

Chart 3   Integration of key social service functions

It is worth remembering Henry Ford's maxim 'you can have any colour, as long as it is black'. I would contend that social services not that long ago delivered along those lines. All individual needs were railroaded into day care or residential services, whereas now, we approach a time when we can integrate key social service functions to meet the needs of the individual (Chart 3).

The experience of the North Devon pilot project has been difficult and slow to get off the ground, but every piece of work that I have looked at in the Devon pilot projects I believe demonstrates the value of the Initiative rather than highlights its failures.